# Poems about

# me

## A collection of poems about values

Compiled by Brian Moses

Artwork by Michaela Blunden

WAYLAND

**Titles in the series**

Editor: Sarah Doughty
Designer: Tim Mayer

First published in 1998 by
Wayland Publishers Ltd
61 Western Road, Hove
East Sussex, BN3 1JD

**British Library Cataloguing in Publication Data**
Poems about me
    1. Children's poetry, English
    I. Moses, Brian, 1950-  II.  Me
    821.9'14'08'035

ISBN 0 7502 1127 X

Printed and bound by G.Canale & C.S.p.A. Turin

# Contents

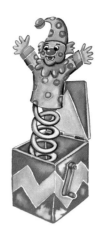

# My place

My school has hundreds of children,
all different shapes and sizes.
The walls are covered with paintings:
the shelves are littered with prizes.
My school has dozens of classrooms,
and I don't know how many doors.
There's a work drawer for every person:
stacks and stacks of drawers.

But there's just one person who has this face,
And sits in this place,
And that's
ME!

*Kate Williams*

# You and your mirror

You gaze in the mirror
and see yourself there.
Long nose, big brown eyes
and curly brown hair.

The mirror can't lie.
What you see there is true,
but perhaps your friends see
a different you.

They see when you're cross
or in a foul mood.
They know when you're hurt,
or angry and rude.

Your best friend sees you
as you really are,
even though you might think
you're an 'Eastenders' star.

So gaze in the mirror
and wonder who's there.
Who's behind those brown eyes
and curly brown hair?

*Wes Magee*

# Wild angry monster

I was shocked by the wild angry monster –
the worst monster anybody could see.
For I stood looking into the mirror
and the wild angry monster was me!

*Charles Thomson*

# I'm special!

In our school
I'm the only one
who can zip around
the playground
at 30 miles an hour!
Watch out everyone. My
wheelchair is supercharged –
I'm special!

In our school
I'm the only one
whose fingers know
how you look, who
never stumbles in the dark.
My eyes are in my fingertips,
my ears pick up every sound –
I'm special!

In our school
I'm the only one
who knows the names
of all the birds
along the riverbank.
I can't write them down,
but I can mimic every call –
I'm special!

In our school
I'm the only one
of me. No-one else
thinks the same, speaks
or looks the same.
In all the world, I'm the only me.
Amazing, when you think of it –
I'm special!

*Moira Andrew*

# It hurts

It hurts when someone makes remarks
About the clothes I wear,
About the foods I refuse to eat
Or the way I cover my hair.

It hurts when someone laughs and jokes
About the way I speak.
"Ignore them," says my Dad, but it's hard
To turn the other cheek.

It hurts when someone calls me names
Because of the colour of my skin.
Everyone's different outside,
But we're all the same within.

*John Foster*

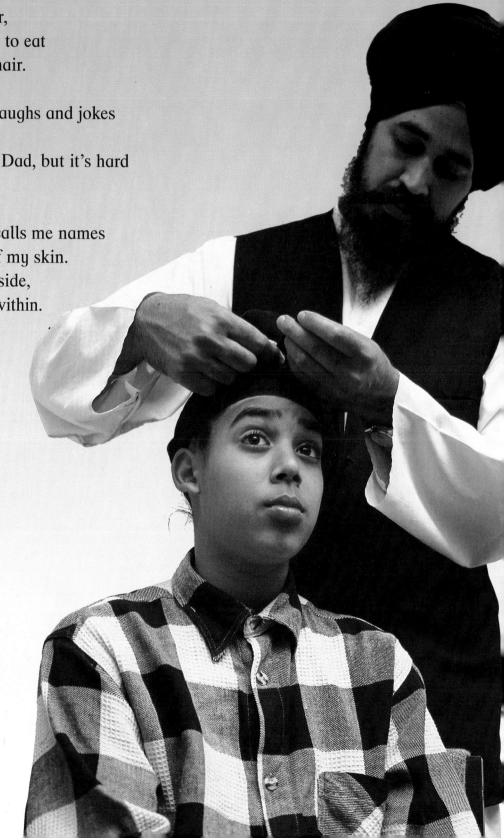

# Give yourself a hug

Give yourself a hug
when you feel unloved

Give yourself a hug
when people put on airs
to make you feel a bug

Give yourself a hug
when everyone seems to give you
a cold-shoulder shrug

Give yourself a hug –
a big big hug

And keep on singing,
'Only one in a million like me
Only one in a million-billion-
  thrillion-zillion
like me.'

*Grace Nichols*

# Skin

Teacher says I have many colours in my skin.
Some colours are thick. Some colours are thin.
I have a bit of everything mixed in ...
browns, whites, blacks, pinks too
some of my veins are a greeny blue.
Teacher said it is a sad fact
that so many people only ever see black.

*Pauline Stewart*

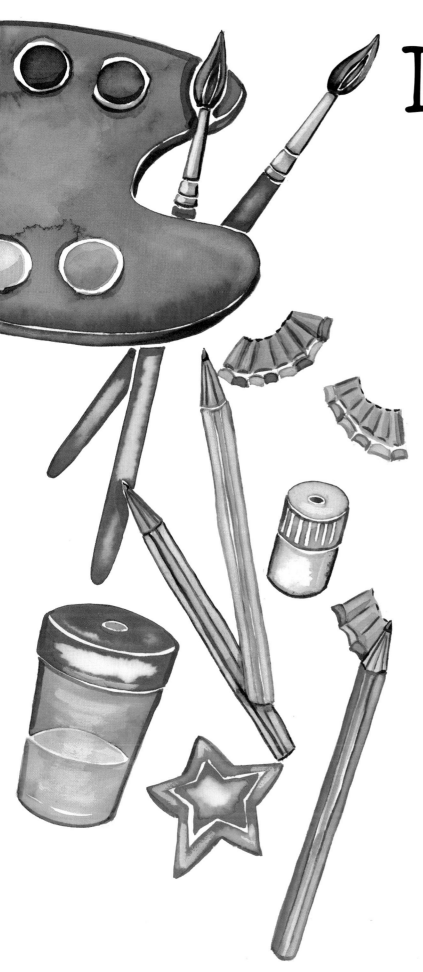

# Ignorance rules

I'm bottom in my school
in maths I never score,
in learning all my tables
my teacher says I'm poor.

My handwriting could be better
my homework's a disgrace,
in every spelling test
I'm always in last place.

But talking I am good at
and for only being nine,
for pulling splinters I'm the best
and falling out of line.

For wriggling in assembly
I'd always win first prize,
and making all the teachers laugh
even though I'm half their size.

For sharpening every pencil
I'd win the silver cup,
and for making sure the paint pots
are always filled right up.

For keeping our room tidy
I'm told that I'm a star,
So why does my report say
I'll never go very far?

*Andrew Collett*

13

# The crowd scene

They say I can't act,
they say I can't dance.
They say I can't sing
but teacher won't give me a chance.

*So I'm in the crowd scene again.*

I asked to be a shepherd,
I begged to be a King.
I said that I'd play any part,
any person, any thing!

*But I'm in the crowd again.*

I wanted to be an angel
but all of Mum's sheets were blue.
I even asked to be Joseph
but Mary said, 'No, not you ...'

*So I'm in the crowd scene again.*

I open and close my mouth,
teacher told me not to sing.
I move from place to place
and I watch and learn everything.

So if ever someone is absent,
I'll know it all by heart.
That's when I'll step from the crowd scene
*to play my proper part.*

*Brian Moses*

# Just because you're my sister

Just because you're my sister,
Why should I do what you do?
Just because you're my sister,
Why should I behave like you?

Everyone goes on and on
About how well you've done,
About the exams you've passed
And all the trophies you've won.

Why can't they leave me alone?
Why can't everyone see
I don't want to be a copy of you,
I just want to be valued as me.

*John Foster*

# Every time

Every time I miss the goal
I'm one step nearer scoring

Every time I drop the ball
my catching skill's improving

Every time I lose a race
My running time gets better

One day I know I'll be the best
But I wish it would happen sooner

*Roger Stevens*

# Growing up

I used to scream and shout
I used to pull my hair,
I used to stamp my feet
if something seemed unfair.

But now I simply smile
now I don't see red,
for now I'm growing up
I just walk away instead.

*Andrew Collett*

Before I was 8
they'd say
(almost every day)
    don't fight, don't hit,
    don't scowl, don't spit.
They'd say
    come in, go out,
    don't scream, don't shout.
They'd say
    sit up, sit down,
    don't fuss, don't frown.
Almost every day
they drove me mad
but now I'm 8
I just feel glad.

Why?
Because they've stopped saying
    don't do this,
    don't do that,
    don't leave those greens,
    don't tease the cat.
Now I'm 8 I'm growing old
and no more am I being told
    don't yap,
    don't slurp,
    don't slouch,
    don't burp.
You know,
being 8
is great!

*Wes Magee*

# Little lies

One day I told a little lie
That grew and grew and grew;
It filled my bedroom and the loft,
The bathroom and the loo.
It squashed itself into the lounge
The kitchen and the hall;
And then slid out under the door
And climbed the garden wall.

It covered gardens, houses, roads,
And then engulfed the city;
It sludged itself on hills and dales
And stopped them looking pretty.
And now I know that little lies
Grow big, just like Mum said;
Don't think I'll tell another one,
I'll try the truth instead.

*Coral Rumble*

# It wasn't me it was him

Uh-oh, I feel the red tide rise and know
My fibbing face is all aglow.
I've blushed bright red
From head to toe.
I cannot meet her beady eye
I look away, I squirm, I sigh ...
I am caught out in a lie
And everyone around can see
My skin is honester than me!

*Jan Dean*

# I told a lie today

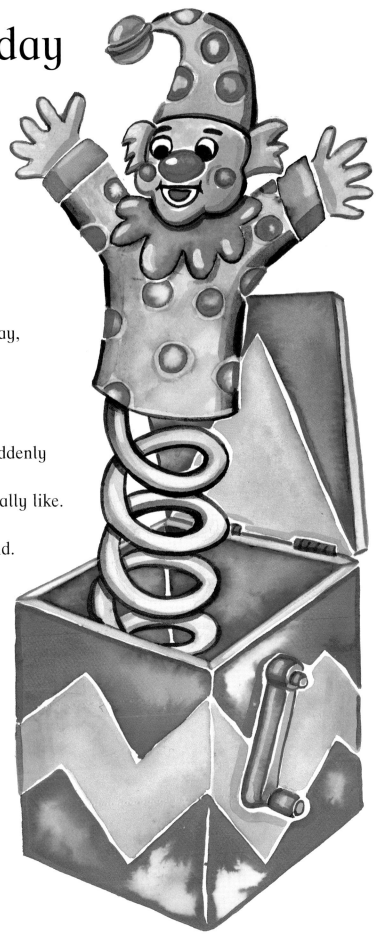

I told a lie today
and it curled up inside me
like a steel hard spring.

It was quite a clever lie,
no one guessed the truth,
they believed me;

but I've carried the twist of it
at the centre of my body, all day,
and I think it's expanding,
filling me up,
making my eyes feel red.

Perhaps it's going to uncoil suddenly
and burst me open,
showing everyone what I'm really like.
I think I had better confess,
before I'm completely unwound.

*Robin Mellor*

# Sorry

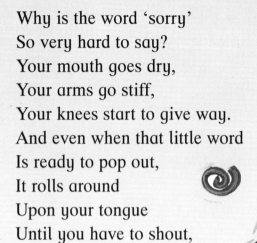

Why is the word 'sorry'
So very hard to say?
Your mouth goes dry,
Your arms go stiff,
Your knees start to give way.
And even when that little word
Is ready to pop out,
It rolls around
Upon your tongue
Until you have to shout,

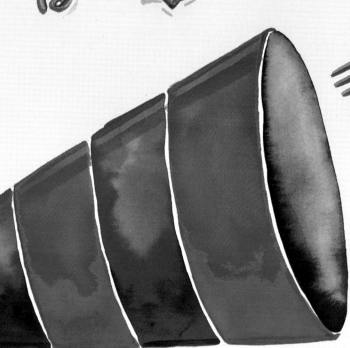

Just to get it past
Your gums, your teeth, your lips
And then your mum says,
"Well, my girl,
It doesn't sound like it!"

*Coral Rumble*

26

# Being good

I used to be bad,
very, very bad!
I used to drive
everyone mad.

I thought at the time
it was very good
when I didn't do
the things that I should,

but it made everyone
so cross and snappy
that even I
became unhappy.

I lay awake
in bed last night
and decided in future
to do things right.

Today I've been
good for so long,
they're asking me now,
'Is anything wrong?'

*Charles Thomson*

27

# Follow your dream

Win the Olympics, be a scientist,
author, acrobat,
fly a balloon.
You can be a pop star, actor, film star,
pilot, astronaut,
go to the moon.

You can sell fridges,
you can build bridges,
you can sail a ship on the seven seas.
Be a physician,
be a politician,
you can be anything you want to be.

Don't listen to the moaners,
knockers, complainers,
you are unique in every way.
Someone will always
try to discourage you,
but you can do it
whatever they say.

Be determined and never give up.
You are much, much better
than you think you are.
All you need is a burning desire.
Follow your dream
and you'll go far.

*Roger Stevens*

# Notes for parents and teachers

It is hoped that the poems in this book will assist children in developing their own self-knowledge and in learning to value their own uniqueness. There should be plenty of time for talking about the poems and discussing how far the ideas expressed relate to children's own circumstances. It is anticipated too, that many of these poems may be presented to children as stimulus or models for their own writing.

Consider the notion of uniqueness in poems such as 'My Place' by Kate Williams, 'I'm Special' by Moira Andrew and 'Just Because You're My Sister' by John Foster. Ask children to identify factors that make an individual unique. How are children unique in their particular families or classroom? They may be able to make a written response based around the phrase, 'I'm the only one who ...'

> In my family, I'm unique,
> I'm the only one who
> wears glasses,
> likes coleslaw,
> clicks fingers.
>
> I'm the only one who
> sleeps with the cat,
> enjoys monopoly,
> likes reading scary stories.

Many of the poems in this collection have patterns where one or more phrases or lines are repeated to help strengthen the rhythm. Can children identify some of these poems e.g. 'I'm Special', 'The Crowd Scene', 'Every Time', 'Give Yourself a Hug'. Some children may enjoy reading these poems aloud and listening to the rhythm. Perhaps they could also be performed with a background of percussion instruments.

Do any children feel the same as the complainer in John Foster's poem? Are they annoyed by constant comparison with another child? Can they write a story based around an argument that develops between a brother and sister, where one of them is being unfavourably compared in this way? Suggest that the story contains plenty of dialogue so that the reader knows exactly what the argument is.

How often do children feel like the subject of Roger Stevens' poem 'Every Time'? Help to foster a positive image by discussing the things that children are good at. Lists can be drawn up alongside a second list, 'Things I'd like to be better at.' Talk about setting goals and how slowly but surely these goals are achievable. When a child has a positive self-image of course, then he or she is more likely to look positively on others.

Read the poems '8' by Wes Magee and 'Growing Up' by Andrew Collett. This could lead to discussion as to how behaviour is modified as children grow. Again children may enjoy writing a poem using a repeating line..

> Once I used to ...
> but now ...

Look at the three poems about telling lies. Point out how the lie grows in 'Little Lies', about how it is portrayed as, '... curled up ... like a steel hard spring' in 'I Told a Lie Today' and the effects of the lie on the liar in 'It Wasn't Me, it was Him.' Can children think of other ways to picture lies – for example, a lie spreads like spilt ink on a tablecloth. They can also consider the possible implications of telling lies through a reading of Aesop's Fable, 'The Boy Who Cried Wolf'. Could this be retold as a story or a poem?

# Books to read

The following books may be useful to use alongside the poems featured in this collection:

"I DON'T CARE!" LEARNING ABOUT RESPECT and "IT WASN'T ME!" LEARNING ABOUT HONESTY by Brian Moses and Mike Gordon (Wayland, 1997).
Everyday situations and humorous illustrations help children answer questions about consideration and honesty.

I LIKE THAT STUFF – POEMS FROM MANY CULTURES edited by Morag Styles (Cambridge University Press, 1984).
The first Section, 'Me, Myself and Others' may prove useful.

THE FIB AND OTHER STORIES by George Layton (Macmillan Children's Books 1997).
A reissue of a book inspired by the author's childhood in the 1950s. The title story 'The Fib' raises many questions about the ethics of telling white lies.

BERNARD'S MAGIC and BERNARD'S PRIZE by Dick Cate (Walker 1997 and 1996).
Uplifting stories that deal with the development of Bernard's self-esteem through a series of funny adventures.

ONCE THERE WERE GIANTS by Martin Waddell and Penny Dale (Walker Books, 1989).
A lovely picture book about growing up and becoming one of the giants!

# Acknowledgements

The author and publishers would like to thank the poets and their agents for allowing their poems to be used in this anthology. Although every attempt has been made to contact the owners, if we have been unable to contact copyright holders we apologise for this apparent negligence.

Picture acknowledgments:
Bubbles 8/9 (Jennie Woodcock), 11 (David Robinson), 24 (Jennie Woodcock); C.F.C.L/ Image Select 14/15 (Chris Fairclough); Tony Stone Worldwide *cover*, 12 and *title page* (Kevin Horan), 17 (Peter Cade), 20 (Mitch Kezar); Zefa 27.

# Index of first lines